RECONSTITUTING THE WORLD
the poetry and vision of Adrienne Rich

by Judith McDaniel

A life I didn't choose
chose me . . .
1961

Only she who says
she did not choose, is the loser in the end.
1976

The will to change dramatically distinguishes the career of Adrienne Rich from many contemporary artists. Accepting at first the roles assigned by society, Rich moved from dutiful daughter/apprentice to mother/creator, excelling–poetically, at least–within the boundaries of her sex, generation and class. At mid-life she began to break out of those boundaries: "Locked in the closet at 4 years old I beat the wall with my body/that act is in me still."[1] Writing poems that were no longer nice, in forms that reflected her mind's straining for new visions, the poet began to challenge, and in recent years her work has reflected her life changes–from daughter-in-law to radical lesbian feminist.[2] The process of this growth is recorded for us in her poetry.

While apparently accepting the traditional female roles in early life, nonetheless feelings of strain and stifled emotion characterize Adrienne Rich's first two volumes.[3] The opening poem in *A Change of World,* "Storm Warnings," sets the tone of both books:

> The glass has been falling all the afternoon,
> And knowing better than the instrument
> What winds are walking overhead, what zone
> Of gray unrest is moving across the land,
> I leave the book upon a pillowed chair
> And walk from window to closed window, watching
> Boughs strain against the sky.

---

[1] Adrienne Rich, *Poems Selected and New* (New York: W.W. Norton and Co., 1975), p.140.

[2] By publishing two poems in the anthology, *Amazon Poetry,* Rich has included herself in the prefatory note which announces that all of these poems "were written by women who define themselves as lesbians. And who have chosen, by publishing their poetry here, to affirm publicly that identity." Joan Larkin and Elly Bulkin, ed., *Amazon Poetry* (New York: Out and Out Books, 1975), p.9.

[3] *A Change of World* (New Haven: Yale University Press, 1951) and *The Diamond Cutters* (New York: Harper and Brothers, 1955).

The controlled iambic rhythm, broken appropriately in the first, fourth, and sixth lines by an anapest as the wind strains against the glass, contains the threat of violent weather, just as the imagined room protects the poet. The form of the poem is a device, used exactly as the drawn curtains and the hurricane lanterns, as a "defense against the season;/ These are the things that we have learned to do/Who live in troubled regions." Another scene of restrained violence follows with "Aunt Jennifer's Tigers" who pace harmlessly across the embroidered tapestry, while her own energy is submerged; she lies "ringed with ordeals she was mastered by." Rich herself was unaware of the tensions her poems illustrate: later she was to write, "In those years formalism was part of the strategy—like asbestos gloves, it allowed me to handle materials I couldn't pick up barehanded."[4] To fill the role of poet, to win the approval of those whom she imitated, Rich had nearly crafted herself out of feeling. Like many of the women she described, these early poems seem nearly suffocated by self-control.

Rich's poetic adaption was not unique. Barbara Bellow Watson, in an essay on women and power, reminds us that

> women, like other groups with minority status, adopt various forms of accommodation to protect themselves. The most essential form of accommodation for the weak is to conceal what power they do have and to avoid anything that looks like threat or competition. [5]

Just as these early poems seldom focused specifically on the woman described, concealing her in metaphors of tapestry, uncharted seas and skies,[6] so too Rich's first expressed asthetic accommodated the power of a masculine school of critical thought. "At a Bach Concert" affirms that "form is the ultimate gift that love can offer" and admonishes, "a too-compassionate art is half an art./Only such proud restraining purity/ Restores the else-betrayed, too human heart." The self-conscious use here of the rhymed form, the frequent hyphens, enclose the meaning in an archaic restraint. The exact meaning of these words must then be carefully extracted. Form, not the more amorphous "craft," is the pre-

---

[4] Adrienne Rich, "When We Dead Awaken: Writing as Re-Vision," *College English,* Vol. 34, no. 1(October, 1972), p. 22.

[5] Barbara Bellow Watson, "On Power and the Literary Text," *Signs: A Journal of Women in Culture and Society,* Vol. I, no. 1 (Autumn, 1975), p. 113.

[6] *Eg.,* "Aunt Jennifer's Tigers," "Mathilde in Norway," "Unsounded," and "For the Conjunction of Two Planets" in *A Change of World.*

ferred value of this early Rich aesthetic. Only through controlled, restraining forms can the emotion be communicated safely. The danger is two-fold. Too great a compassion is sentiment, not art; and the artist may reveal more of herself than is safe for her, or than her critical audience would wish to read. Rich's essential transformation as an artist was a movement away from this aesthetic toward an art that allowed a far more personal expression, allowed her to take risks as a poet and a compassionate woman.

Snapshots of a Daughter-in-Law,[7] published eight years after Rich's second volume, marks a significant change in style and attitude. The title of the volume is personal; it also emphasizes an awareness of her role within the forms of marriage. She is no longer the young woman who could change her world arbitrarily, nor the poet whose craft is compared to that of the diamond cutter.

> The poem was jotted in fragments during children's
> naps, brief hours in a library, or at 3 a.m. after
> rising with a wakeful child. I despaired of doing
> any continuous work at this time. Yet I began to feel
> that my fragments and scraps had a common consciousness
> and a common theme, one which I would have been very
> unwilling to put on paper at an earlier time because
> I had been taught that poetry should be "universal,"
> which meant, of course, non-female.[8]

Here, the poet is a mother/wife/daughter-in-law whose life is given over to others, and that circumstance significantly affects her subject and, increasingly, the form of her poem. At times, the numbering of the sections within the title poem seems the only controlling factor, argument and syntax giving the reader little direction.

In "Snapshots of a Daughter-in-Law" Rich shows us a young woman who is beginning to realize that her identity is not that of the women she has been given as models: "Nervy, glowering, your daughter/wipes the teaspoons, grows another way." Like Joan of Arc, this protagonist hears voices; but hers bid her not to sacrifice herself: "Have no patience . . . Be insatiable . . . Save yourself; others you cannot save." These are not the voices of angels, but of monsters, the inevitable accompaniment

[7] *Snapshots of a Daughter-in-Law* (New York: W.W. Norton & Co., 1963).
[8] "When We Dead Awaken," p. 24.

of growing self-awareness and self-involvement for women. And these monsters do not come from another sphere; they are from within: "A thinking woman sleeps with monsters./The beak that grips her, she becomes."

No specific political connections enlighten the protagonist of this poem. Rich celebrates those several predecessors who remained strong and produced their writing, such as Mary Wolstonecraft, Emily Dickinson, but the future is vague and awkwardly expressed:

> Well,
> she's long about her coming, who must be
> more merciless to herself than history.
> Her mind full to the wind, I see her plunge
> breasted and glancing through the currents,
> at least as beautiful as any boy
> or helicopter,
>
> poised, still coming,
> her fine blades making the air wince
>
> but her cargo
> no promise then:
> delivered
> palpable
> ours.

The image of the helicopter represents both power and deliverance and its blades are weapon-like. But the ludicrous shape, the emphasis on a technological rather than natural event, make this leap of the imagination a far-fetched one. What we wish to belive is the wistful voice at the poem's end: a promise of selfhood that is "delivered," "palpable" and "ours." The theme of the poem is the role of a woman poet; the problem, in 1969, was one of inadequate models for that mode of female achievement.

While the political perspective of *Snapshots of a Daughter-in-Law* is nebulous, Rich does attempt in this volume to discuss, if not resolve, the problem she must have seen in applying her previously stated aesthetic to this new style of writing. "The Roofwalker" compares the poet to a construction worker balanced precariously on a rafter, "exposed, larger than life,/ and due to break my neck." The female poet has labored "with infinite exertion" and succeeded in laying "a roof I can't live under." Her exertions were thwarted because "A life I didn't choose/ chose me"—the life this volume depicts of mother, wife and daughter[9]—and thwarted because "even/my tools are the wrong ones/for what I have to do." Rich is not specific, may not be sure herself, whether those wrong tools are the problem of gender identification—a woman writing in a man's voice and poetic form—or simply the problem of a formal style which made writing difficult with infants to care for. But both are connected to the use of a language which the poet is finding increasingly awkward. The phenomena Rich wishes to describe—a new female identity, the nuances of a male/female relationship—make impossible demands on a limited and sexist vocabulary. This combination, the wrong tools and the need to build, leave the poet exposed and vulnerable. Taking chances in her writing, the poet sees herself "naked, ignorant,/a naked man fleeing/across the roofs." With only a small difference, however, with a little less existential courage or curiosity, she could reduce these impulses to mere fantasies, daydreams, instead of her own reality. She could

> be sitting in the lamplight
> against the cream wallpaper
> reading—not with indifference—
> about a naked man
> fleeing across the roofs.

The debate between the possibility of actively engaging in change, or passively watching others take those risks, is the keynote of this volume. In "Prospective Immigrants Please Note" Rich presents the challenge directly:

> Either you will
> go through this door
> or you will not go through.
>
> If you go through
> there is always the risk
> of remembering your name.

---

[9] "My husband spoke eagerly of the children we would have; my parents-in-law awaited the birth of their grandchild. I had no idea of what I wanted, what I could or could not choose." Adrienne Rich, *Of Woman Born: Motherhood as Experience and Institution* (New York: W.W. Norton & Co., 1976), p.25.

Rich tries to present both options fairly: "If you do not go through/ it is possible/to live worthily." But she will not let the reader escape the reality that to refuse growth and change inevitably means that "much will blind you/much will evade you/at what cost who knows?" The matter-of-fact tone of these short terse lines suggests forcibly that Rich herself has gone through the door.

This choice necessarily separates Adrienne Rich from many of her female antecedents–from Christina Rossetti and Emily Dickinson,[10] certainly. A condition of their art required them to choose isolation, to close the door rather than pass through it. Her decision to encounter the self in the world allies her–emotionally and poetically–with several of her contemporaries. "The Roofwalker," for example is dedicated to Denise Levertov and seems to be a response to Levertov's "From the Roof" in which a woman bringing in the wash on her Manhattan rooftop becomes the transformer and the transformed, watching and taking part in the sensuous, teeming life beneath her. And Rich experiences in this volume a problem of voice similar to that which plagued Levertov. In the fifties and sixties it was difficult for a woman to escape the fact that poet was a masculine noun. In Levertov's prose piece, "The Poet in the World," in a grotesque and awkward allegory, the female poet gives birth to a male child who becomes the poet-he, who then goes into the world to experience it. Similarly, in "Snapshots of a Daughter-in-Law" the standard of beauty and achievement is still male. The woman of the future, Rich tells us, will be "at least as beautiful as any boy."

Snapshots of a Daughter-in-Law was a book ignored by the critics, written off, Rich says, as "being too bitter and personal." In her next book she retreated from those earlier insights: ". . . something in me was saying, 'If my material, my subject matter as a woman is going to be denied me, then there is only one other subject for me and that is death.' That's why *Necessities of Life*[11] is a book about death."[12] And it is why *Leaflets*[13] is permeated with anger, diffused nervous tension and un-

[10] "I read the older women poets with their peculiar keeness and ambivalence: Sappho, Christina Rossetti, Emily Dickinson . . . I know that my style was formed first by male poets: by the men I was reading as an undergraduate–Frost, Dylan Thomas, Donne, Auden, MacNiece, Stevens, Yeats." in "When We Dead Awaken" p. 21.

[11] *Necessities of Life* (New York: W.W. Norton & Co., 1966).

[12] "Adrienne Rich and Robin Morgan Talk About Poetry and Women's Culture," *The New Woman's Survival Sourcebook,* ed. Susan Rennie and Kirsten Grimstad (New York: Alfred Knopf, 1975), p. 107.

[13] *Leaflets* (New York: W.W. Norton & Co., 1969).

focussed hostility. *Leaflets* opens with "Orion;" the you addressed in the poem is the poet herself, "the active principle, the energetic imagination."[14] This aspect of her personality, that energy and self involvement out of which the poetry is written, is on the defensive and will fight for its life:

> Breathe deep! No hurt, no pardon
> out here in the cold with you
> You with your back to the wall.

That image of defiant extremity recurs and becomes more specific: "Did you think I was talking about my life?/I was trying to drive a tradition up against the wall." And finally, "I can't live at the hems of that tradition–/will I last to try the beginning of the next?" The tradition that is forcing her to the wall, forcing her to live and write on its outskirts, is patriarchy and this is specifically recognized in Rich's restatement of the theme of Auden's "Musee Des Beaux Arts." Auden insisted that "About suffering they were never wrong,/The Old Masters: how well they understood/Its human position." Rich sees that the scenes haven't changed, "We stand in the porch,/two archaic figures: a woman and a man." But her perspective on suffering is unique: "The old masters, the old sources/ haven't a clue what we're about." She is not, as one critic suggested with irritation, declaring "human experience in general is so radically disparate that even the old masters could fail to intimate our problems, provide us with a clue."[15] She *is* insisting the old masters, the patriarchy, have cut themselves off from the female experience; as her own sense of herself as a woman who has been forced to the edges of male culture becomes more conscious, she realizes how little that culture represents her own needs and desires.

Like the four-year-old flinging herself against the closet door, the images in *Leaflets* strike out against that cultural entombment. Blood, fire and war converge in the repeated identification of the poet with the red fox:

---

[14] "When We Dead Awaken," p. 24.

[15] Robert Boyers, "On Adrienne Rich: Intelligence and Will," *Salmagundi,* 22-3 (Spring-Summer, 1973), p. 140.

The fox, panting, fire-eyed
gone to earth in my chest.
How beautiful we are,
she and I, with our auburn
pelts, our trails of blood,
our miracle escapes,
our whiplash panic flogging us on
to new miracles.

In "5:30 A.M." Rich is sure that she and the fox will die, the hunters, "inanely single-minded/will have our skins at last." In "Abnegation" the woman poet and the vixen share a common birthright: ". . . No archives,/no heirlooms, no future/except death."

"No future/except death" is a distinct recognition by Adrienne Rich of the aesthetics expressed by the "confessional poets."[16] But Rich's identification with the confessional poets is not complete. In "On Edges" words appear indicating Sylvia Plath is the source of this reverie/nightmare: "dressing-gowns," "monster," "lampshade." Still, Rich is a translator who, taking a "torn letter," can not "fit these ripped-up flakes together." She recognizes and agrees that "the blades on that machine / could cut you to ribbons." The blades are not the dangerous helicopter blades from "Snapshots of a Daughter-in-Law," but the relentless keys of the poet's typewriter. And the "delicate hooks, scythe-curved intentions/you and I handle," are, in this poem of Rich's, words–in a literal sense, commas, the expression of a hesitation or silence. The last two poems of Sylvia Plath's life were "Edge" and "Words." "Words" are the axe's edge for Plath; "words dry and riderless" take on a life of their own, endangering the poet's life. Rich is willing to acknowledge this danger, to become the renegade:

. . . I'd rather
taste blood, yours or mine, flowing
from a sudden slash, than cut all day
with blunt scissors on dotted lines
like the teacher told.

Rich echoes Plath's "the blood jet is poetry." But that which differentiates her from the confessional poets is her insistence that poetry/

[16] For example, Sylvia Plath, Anne Sexton, John Berryman, Robert Lowell.

words/language have a "function" that "is humane." Adrienne Rich will encounter the danger, but her belief in a direction for the future will allow her to survive that encounter.

In *Leaflets,* then, Rich connects the problem of survival to the problem of communication: a primary theme of her mature poetry. "Tell me what you are going through," the man asks in "Leaflets," but "the attention flickers" and he cannot hear her response, cannot hear her plead, "know that I exist." The words she tries to write in the "Ghazals" are "vapor-trails of a plane that has vanished" and she implores the reader, "When you read these lines, think of me/and of what I have not written here." In the last "Ghazal," dedicated to her husband, she wishes for some magic incantation to protect them from the suffering they will have to endure, and she asks him, speaking "as a woman to a man/. . . How did we get caught up fighting this forest fire,/we, who were only looking for a still place in the woods?"

Within a year, Rich wrote a poem that begins to analyze politically that question: "how did we get caught?" "Tear Gas"[17] announces:

> The will to change begins in the body not in the mind
> My politics is in my body, accruing and expanding with every
> act of resistance and each of my failures.

The subjective physical self is now seen as the focus for profound political change. Economically, a woman's body has always been a political object, controlled by a man, a master, a religion or a government. This new war will not be over until the woman can assert control over her own destiny, physical and cultural. To achieve both, she needs

> . . . a language to hear myself with
> to see myself in
> a language like pigment released on the board
> blood-black, sexual green, reds
> veined with contradictions
> bursting under pressure from the tube
> staining the old grain of the wood.

The tensions here are palpable and explosive and the language seems inadequate. Rich protests, "but this is not what I mean/these images are not what I mean." It will be years before women find the images they

---

[17] First published in *Poems Selected and New,* 1975.

need for this expression; but Rich now knows the direction of the search. She is moving "toward a place where we can no longer be together" as men and women; she is moving toward "another kind of action."

To effect this journey to a new place, a new action, Rich must first create a new language, a new way to express woman's experience. The task is enormous, but not impossible; for she means to shape this new language, not through new words, but through new perceptions, so that we may first see ourselves in the new place. The old language causes pain, suffering, and isolation because it does not acknowledge or portray the human situation in a truthful way. One corrective, insists Rich, when "we are confronted with the naked and unabashed failure of patriarchal politics and patriarchal civilization," is to make an accurate record of human feelings by rewriting the stories and myths that purport to represent our deepest reality. And she is determined that "the sexual myths underlying the human condition can and shall be recognized and changed."[18] *The Will to Change*[19] and *Diving into the Wreck*[20] represent a sophisticated and passionate attempt to give us a new vision of ourselves. These volumes recognize that myths and legends have had a complex interrelationship with the development of civilization and the concommitant development of the consciousness of the self. Rich returns again and again to images of mankind's pre-historic and pre-conscious state and then carefully leads us toward a new and altered perception. The process is one of rebirth and conscious recreation.

The Will to Change opens with a poem that moves us carefully back into a state where "the last absolutes were torn to pieces." The image of "November 1968" is an incinerator of autumn leaves, the smoke from which begins "to float free/... the unleafed branches won't hold you/nor the radar aerials." The smokey essence of the leaves, drifting into the air and disappearing, becomes a metaphor for the human return to a preconscious state in which the self and the environment are one, before the individual begins to differentiate itself from the group or its surroundings. As the poet watches this process–individual leaves merging into smoke–she wonders:

> How you broke open, what sheathed you
> until this moment
> I know nothing about it
> my ignorance of you amazes me.

[18] "Preface," *Poems Selected and New,* p. xv-xvi.
[19] *The Will to Change* (New York: W.W. Norton and Co., 1971).
[20] *Diving into the Wreck* (New York: W.W. Norton and Co., 1973).

"Study of History" charts the vagaries of human development when it is not consciously controlled. The poem describes a river at night. Lights on the shore opposite the viewer are occasionally blotted out by the "unseen hulls" of passing barges. The viewer cannot see the barges, only knows that the lights go out and then reappear. Cause and effect cannot be determined. Here, the river is formed, irrevocably and inexplicably, it would seem. And the poet, "lying in the dark, to think of you," reminds herself that this place is not the origin of the river and that

> . . . we have never entirely
> known what was done to you upstream
> what powers trepanned
> which of your channels diverted.

Like any human personality, those early processes and boundaries that form the present are only visible as an occasional light winking on and off.

Rich's most straightforward attempt to present a corrective to "what was done to you upstream" is "Planetarium" in which she attempts to rewrite some of the myths and legends which have misrepresented woman's potential. It is a poem, she says, "in which at last the woman in the poem and the woman writing the poem become the same person. . . It was written after a visit to a real planetarium, where I read an account of the work of Caroline Herschel, the astronomer, who worked with her brother William, but whose name remained obscure, as his did not."[21] What Caroline Herschel saw changed our earthly vision of the sky—"What we see, we see / and seeing is changing"—and the poet sees Caroline Herschel and gives the reader a new way of seeing a female reality. Rich knows that all of our lives we have been "bombarded" by the old myths about women, women "doing penance for impetuousness." Those messages reach all of us, always:

> I have been standing all my life in the
> direct path of a battery of signals
> the most accurately transmitted most
> untranslatable language in the universe.

But in this poem, the poet, like the astronomer, becomes an active

---

[21] "When We Dead Awaken," p. 25

agent of change. No longer the passive receptacle of other's descriptions of her,

> . . . I am an instrument in the shape
> of a woman trying to translate pulsations
> into images   for the relief of the body
> and the reconstruction of the mind.

Her theme is the will to change; the very conscious reappraisal of Caroline Herschel suggests one direction for this change: "Writing as re-vision."[22]

"The Burning of Paper Instead of Children" attempts a much more difficult process of change. It is a poem about language, and once again we sense a real ambivalance here toward the power of the written word, which Rich both denies and affirms. The headnote of the poem quotes Daniel Berrigan, on trial in Baltimore for burning draft records: "I was in danger of verbalizing my moral impulses out of existence." And the poem itself is a verbalization of the poet's own moral impulses about her sense of her function and purpose in a violent society.

The first section of the poem asserts that the symbolic act (burning a book) is less important to the poet than the burning of a child, or Joan of Arc. Yet she learns of Joan's martydom in a book, *The Trial of Jeanne d'Arc,* and is so mesmerized by the telling of the story that "they take the book away / because I dream of her too often." This irony—the paradox of the power of words vs. the power of action—runs through the poem. The poet reads the knowledge which allows an identification with Joan of Arc, and she concludes part one of the poem with the realization, "I *know* it hurts to burn [emphasis mine]."

To imagine a time of "silence" is the attempt of the second section, and the poet proposes communication through touch. Physical love allows a "relief / from this tongue   this slab of limestone / or reinforced concrete." Verbalization is a gravestone, as the Indians discovered who, in the poet's imagination, communicated "in signals of smoke" until "knowledge of the oppressor" gave them language. The ambivalence of the poem is never more profoundly realized than in the terse conclusion of this section: "This is the oppressor's language / yet I need it to talk to you."

The poem does not conclude in the fifth and final section, it ignites. The languages of Frederick Douglas and Jeanne d'Arc were "pure" because their languages and their actions coincided; their languages were

---

22 The subtitle of the essay, "When We Dead Awaken: Writing as Re-Vision."

their actions: thus, "a language is a map of our failures" and our successes. This is the knowledge that will incite human change. With the realization that "I cannot touch you now," that earlier hope of a personal, physical communication is negated:

> I am in danger. You are in danger. The burning
> of a book arouses no sensation in me. I know it
> hurts to burn. There are flames of napalm in
> Catonsville, Maryland. I know it hurts to burn.
> The typewriter is overheated, my mouth is burning,
> I cannot touch you and this is the oppressor's
> language.

"My politics," Rich had written earlier, "is in my body." When we realize how inextricably related are all of our modes of expression, the lives we live become integrated into new political potential. She shows its complexity to us:

> Trying to tell the doctor where it hurts
> like the Algerian
> who walked from his village burning
>
> his whole body a cloud of pain
> and there are no words for this
>
> except himself.

In this single image Rich unites the words, the pain, the body, and the politic. A vivid example of her poetic imagination, the precise visualization of an abstraction is a technique she has perfected as a mature poet, and will continue to use.

Each of the poems in *The Will to Change* is a further commentary on this political reality, from the myth of Orpheus as it is rewritten by Eurydice to the more specific directions in "Shooting Script." The penultimate section of the poem returns to the image of the river from "Study of History." Now the poet is not a silent observer on the shore of the river; she is on the river, although "once it would not have occurred to / me to put out in a boat, not on a night like this." Now, she is encountering life, having chosen to go through the door of life changes, and part of this choice includes pledging "myself to try any / instrument that came my way. Never to refuse one from conviction / of incompetence." Learning new ways is not easy and again we are reminded that the old life gave women the "wrong tools" for the task: "I had no / special training and my own training was against me." Still, she is out on the moving river. "I watched the lights on the shore I had left for a long time; each / one, it seemed to me, was a light I might have lit, in the old days." It is a process she describes as pulling "yourself up by your own roots."

In the poems that followed *The Will to Change,* Rich continued to focus on these three problems: changing the language, rewriting the myths, and returning to the sources from which our conscious actions originate. The poems about language are characterized by anger and frustration. The first poem in *Diving Into the Wreck* is titled "Trying to Talk With a Man" and the experience is compared to testing bombs. "The Phenomenology of Anger" finds words and images to describe a rage so profound it could lead to "Madness. Suicide. Murder./ Is there no way out but these?" When she dreams of meeting her enemy, she imagines acetylene

> raking his body down to the thread
> of existence
> burning away his lie
> leaving him in a new
> world; a changed
> man.

This anger, Rich says, is not female hysteria. It has real sources in the daily existence of women:

> Today, much poetry by women–and prose for that matter–is charged with anger. I think we need to go through that anger, and we will betray our own reality if we try, as Virginia Woolf was trying, for an objectivity, a detachment . . . Both the victimization and the anger experienced by women are real, and have real sources, everywhere in the environment, built into society.[23]

In other prose writing, Rich began at this time (1972) to articulate more specifically a political perspective that elaborated the insights of her poems. She understands patriarchy as "any kind of group organization in which males hold dominant power and determine what part females

---

[23] "When We Dead Awaken," p. 25.

shall and shall not play,"[24] Not only is this artificial restraint a source of anger to women, Rich finds that

> men—in so far as they are embodiments of the patriarchal idea—have become dangerous to children and other living things, themselves included; and that we can no longer afford to keep the female principle—the mother in all women and the woman in many men—straitened within the tight little postindustrial family, or within any male-induced notion of where the female principle is valid and where it is not.[25]

In those poems in which she is trying to rewrite some of the old myths and stories, Rich is very consciously trying to combat this tendency of the patriarchy. She will not let Orpheus's failure of direction limit her, "a woman in the prime of life." She wants women to "explore the condition of connectedness as a woman. Which is something absolutely new, unique historically, and which is finally so much more life-enhancing"[26] than exploring the condition of woman's alienation. In "Translations" the narrator has become aware that women need not compete and become enemies over a man's affections. They are ignorant that "this way of grief / is shared, unnecessary / and political." It is political because of the unequal power held by the man. Again, in "From a Survivor" Rich's narrator addresses a man with whom she had made "the ordinary pact / of men and women in those days." She has a new vision of that pact, no longer accepts the myth that he can define or control her. His body "is no longer / the body of a god / or anything with power over my life." Her new life is "a succession of brief, amazing movements / each one making possible the next."

"Diving into the Wreck" is Rich's most complex use of an image of rebirth. This time her tools are carefully chosen: she has "read the book of myths, / and loaded the camera,/ and checked the edge of the knifeblade." It is necessary to know the old stories before embarking on a journey to change them. This journey is to record the sources of our origin, hence the camera. The knife is less obvious, until one remembers Rich's frequent earlier warnings—that the journey is dangerous.

---

[24] "The Anti-Feminist Woman," in *Adrienne Rich's Poetry,* ed. Barbara C. Gelpi and Albert Gelpi (New York: W. W. Norton and Co., 1975), p. 101.

[25] "The Anti-Feminist Woman," p. 104-5.

[26] "Adrienne Rich and Robin Morgan Talk About Poetry," p. 106.

As the narrator descends, the water turns from blue to green to black. There is the effect of "blacking out," becoming unconscious, while still remaining in control. As she begins to move in this new element, the swimmer learns that "the sea is not a question of power." It is, rather, the all encompassing "deep element" in which she must learn "to turn my body without force." She has come "to explore the wreck. . ./ to see the damage that was done / and the treasures that prevail." The wreck is a layered image: it is the life of one woman, the source of successes and failures; it is the history of all women submerged in a patriarchal culture; it is that source of myths about male and female sexuality which shape our lives and roles today. Whichever, the swimmer came for "the wreck and not the story of the wreck / the thing itself and not the myth." She explores the wreck and records for us her experiences of the cargo, "the half-destroyed instruments . . . the water-eaten log / the fouled compass." But no questions are answered here for those who have not found their own way to this place; we are given no explanation for why the wreck occurred. Nor is there any account of the swimmer's return, the use to which she puts this new information. It is as if Rich still found herself in the dilemma at the end of "Snapshots of a Daughter-in-Law" when it seemed impossible to record an image of the "new woman." Indeed, she said in 1974, two years after "Diving into the Wreck,"

> I absolutely cannot imagine what it would be like to be a woman in a non patriarchal society. At moments I have this little glimmer of it. When I'm in a group of women, where I have a sense of real energy flowing and of power in the best sense–not power of domination, but just access to sources–I have some sense of what that could be like. But it's very rare that I can imagine even that.[27]

"From an Old House in America," published in 1975, irrevocably makes Adrienne Rich's connection with the lives of other women. Thinking of Emily Bronte in her life long isolation, she writes: "I place my hand on the hand / of the dead, invisible palm-print / on the doorframe." In the poem she reaches out "to comprehend a miracle beyond /

[27] "Three Conversations, " in *Adrienne Rich's Poetry,* p.119.

raising the dead: the undead to watch / back on the road of birth." The road, for American women, has been grotesquely difficult; and in a series of breathtaking vignettes Rich does indeed look back on the road to watch her own birth. Slaves, witches, pioneers, women chained together, hung together, or dying alone, whatever the history of individual lives has been, each was a victim of a power that took her life out of her own control. Finally, for the poet, after the repression, murder, exploitation characterizing these women's lives, she finds:

> A dream of tenderness
>
> wrestles with all I know of history
> I cannot now lie down
>
> with a man who fears my power
> or reaches for me as for death
>
> or with a lover who imagines
> we are not in danger.

The implications of this declaration are clear: the dream of tenderness is in loving other women. The mind leaps back to the earlier assertion in "The Phenomenology of Anger:"

> "The only real love I have ever felt
> was for children and other women.
> Everything else was lust, pity,
> self-hatred, pity, lust."
> This is a woman's confession.

As a poet and a feminist, Adrienne Rich knows that she must live a life that allows her to make connections with other women, connections which will unite her inner reality and her outer environment.

In her two most recent books Adrienne Rich explores the potential for woman's power. Her prose work, *Of Woman Born: Motherhood as Experience and Institution,* shows that potential interfaced against the dark power of the patriarchy. She writes of women's quest "for models or blueprints of female power which shall be neither replications of male power nor carbon-copies of the male stereotype of the powerful, controlling destructive woman."[28] She asks vindication for the belief "that patriarchy is in some ways a degeneration, that women exerting power would use it differently from men: nonpossessively, nonviolently, nondestructively."[29] *Dream of a Common Language*[30] opens with a poem entitled "Power." The complexities of this power are inherent in the story of Marie Curie who discovered the vital properties of uranium, and who died from radiation poisoning, "denying / her wounds came from the same source as her power." Marie Curie did not know–literally–how to handle power. Once again Rich's poetic image–the woman holding in her "suppurating" fingers the test-tube of uranium, source of energy and death–unites the abstract and political difficulties of power.

"Phantasia for Elvira Shatayev" further explores the danger of accepting and using power. In this poem the women's climbing team dies in an attempt on a mountain, dies, in the words of the team leader, while seeing in the struggle "my own forces so taken up and shared / and given back" by each of the women on the team. Nothing is lost. They lose their lives. But each of us must die and these women know now "we have always been in danger / down in our separateness . . . but till now/ we had not touched our strength." They will choose to survive only to live a life of their own choosing: "We will not live / to settle for less." But they will not die, living in Adrienne Rich's poem as the poet assumes the voice of Shatayev, taking up her vision and sharing it, giving back to the women who died a new kind of life. The climb and the poem are a communal endeavor.

Language, poetry, contains a power of its own. And the poet has a responsibility to that power, to the power of consciousness, self-awareness and growth. "Origins and History of Consciousness" is a poem about Adrienne Rich's life long commitment to poetry. We enter the space in which she creates, share her process of analyzing and testing each idea that enters a poem. Writing poetry has always been a life-serious undertaking for this woman:

> No one lives in this room
> without confronting the whiteness of the wall
> behind the poems, planks of books,
> photographs of dead heroines.
> Without contemplating last and late
> the true nature of poetry. The drive
> to connect. The dream of a common language.

---

[28] "The Kingdom of the Fathers," *Partisan Review* XLIII, no. 1 (Spring, 1975), p. 25. This section appeared in a prepublication excerpt of *Of Woman Born,* but was not included in final publication.
[29] *Of Woman Born,* p. 72.
[30] *Dream of a Common Language* (New York: W.W. Norton and Co., 1978).

The necessities of a larger world call the poet (and reader) out of the drama of the intensely personal—"the drive / to connect"—to an integration of the personal and the larger political realities. It is this necessity, finally, that has brought Rich's poetic voice beyond that range explored by the confessional poets. "Even in her most personal lyrics," critics have recognized, she "stretches all human activities on the frame of social and political consciousness."[31] Her poetry

> does not solely rely upon an . . . emotional relationship to the poet and the poetic vision. Adrienne Rich's poetry maintains its autonomy, states its case, evolves its arguments, and at all times relates the personal to the objective, temporal, timeless, to the universal. Adrienne Rich never avoids either interior or exterior examination, never takes a stand that is not consciously chosen and firmly reinforced. Her poetry engages its subject; no conclusion is gained without a test.[32]

Within the later poems, this testing occurs more and more frequently in the use of dialogue, quotations (as in the journal segments from "Phantasia for Elvira Shatayev" or the letter fragments in "Paula Becker to Clara Westhoff") and the accrual of emotion and meaning in the repeated use of a particular image.

A silent beast, for example, stalks through *The Dream of a Common Language,* but the image is not new for Rich. The very early poem, "Aunt Jennifer's Tigers," the gorillas of "The Observer," Rich's identification with the hunted fox in *The Will to Change,* have all prepared for our encounter with Rich's image of incipient power, our sleeping "dumb beast, head on her paws, in the corner." In "Splittings" the beast is the pain of self-separation inflicted by the expectations of a patriarchal culture. And, "what kind of beast would turn its life into words?" asks "Love Poem VII," drawing on the expectation and fear of the power of self-revelation. The caged beast (or the empty cage) surfaces in image after image, as in "Natural History" or in "Mother-Right" when the mother and child run from the father/oppressor, "the woman   eyes sharpened in the light/heart stumbling   making for the open."

The beast becomes manifest in "The Lioness." Like women, she

---

[31] Willard Spiegelman, "Voice of the Survivor: The Poetry of Adrienne Rich," *Southwest Review* (Autumn, 1975), p. 386.

[32] Mary Titus, *Adrienne Rich's Poetic Process,* Unpublished senior thesis, Skidmore College (Spring, 1978), p. 66.

knows more than she has experienced. The poet addresses her:

> "In country like this," I say, "the problem is always
> one of straying too far, not of staying
> within bounds. There are caves
> high rocks, you don't explore. Yet you know
> they exist." Her proud, vulnerable head
> sniffs toward them. It is her country, she
> knows they exist.

The poet stands watching the lioness and although she sees much from that perspective, sees that the power of the beast is "half-abnegated" and that "three square years/ encompass where she goes," there is no overt recognition that the lioness is caged. Standing on the outside, looking perhaps between the bars, the poet naturally sees only the lioness. It is a partial vision: not true. The poet must learn more than sympathy; she must be able to enter the lioness's frame of reference, and this she does:

> I look into her eyes
> as one who loves can look,
> entering the space behind her eyeballs,
> leaving myself outside.
> So, at last, through her pupils,
> I see what she is seeing . . .

From inside, the cage, of course, is visible. The lioness knows what lies in the distance—freedom, "the volcano veiled in rainbow"—and she sees what is immediately before her, that which was not strikingly visible from the outside:

> a pen that measures three yards square.
> Lashed bars.
> The cage.
> The penance.

The poet now sees and understands those elements that create the oppression of one who is like and unlike her.

"Hunger," dedicated to Audre Lorde, is the poem in this volume that deals most specifically with these elements of oppression. Adrienne Rich sees the desolation, the wasteland that encompasses a large part of the female experience. Once again, she sees at first from her own limitations, seeing "in my Western skin,/ my Western vision," a landscape that is alien:

> huts strung across a drought-stretched land
> not mine, dried breasts, mine and not mine, a mother
> watching my children shrink with hunger.

The transition here is subtle, but encompassing. The land is *not hers,* the breasts are *"mine* and *not mine,"* but they are *"my* children [emphasis mine]." The involvement is complete and necessary. Because Rich says, if they can convince us that "our pain belongs in some order," that, for example, some of us will suffer a little, and some of us will suffer more because they are more powerless, or black or lesbian, and that's just the way it is, then "They *can* rule the world." We are separated from one another and powerless as long as suffering can be "quantified," as long as the question can be asked:

> Is death by famine worse than death by suicide,
> than a life of famine and suicide, if a black lesbian dies,
> if a white prostitute dies, if a woman genius
> starves herself to feed others,
> self-hatred battening on her body?

Adrienne Rich also knows that no analysis of the problem of hunger by a white middle class American can be separated from one's own sense of class guilt, of passivity—even when that passivity stems from the knowledge that circumstances are so complex that one person of good will can do little or nothing to effect change. "I stand convicted by all my convictions," Rich confesses, "you, too." We will not, she says, accept the responsibility of our vision:

> We shrink from touching
> our power, we shrink away, we starve ourselves
> and each other, we're scared shitless
> of what it could be to take and use our love,
> hose it on a city, on a world,
> to wield and guide its spray, destroying
> poisons, parasites, rats, viruses—
> like the terrible mothers we long and dread to be.

But our failure, the failure of women and mothers and lesbians and all of those whose very existence depends on maintaining a precarious balance, is a failure of nerve: "even our intimacies are rigged with terror," and we confess this, as our "guilt at least is open." Our powers are expended on the struggle to survive and "to hand a kind of life on to our children/ to change reality for our lovers."

Other failures are more damning:

> The decision to feed the world
> is the real decision. No revolution
> has chosen it. For that choice requires
> that women shall be free.

The words are deceptively simple; there are no images. The tone is matter-of-fact, straightforward. There are three simple statements and the connections which lead to their conclusion have everything to say about a feminist apprehension of power, the failures and necessities of power relationships.

The center of *Dream of a Common Language* is a group of lesbian love poems, originally published as a separate booklet[33] and reanthologized here. It is an appropriate choice for continuing the theme of power, for in these poems Rich shows us a glimpse of the power generated by love, specifically the love of women for women:

> You've kissed my hair
> to wake me. "I dreamed you were a poem,"
> I say, "a poem I wanted to show someone . . ."
> and I laugh and fall dreaming again
> of the desire to show you to everyone I love,
> to move openly together
> in the pull of gravity, which is not simple,
> which carries the feathered grass a long way down the upbreathing air.

There is a special recognition in "your small hands, precisely equal to my own," the recognition that "in these hands / I could trust the world." The strength in these poems is the discovery of the self in another, the range of knowing and identification that seems most possible in same-sex love: the encounter of another's pain, for example, leaves the poet knowing "I was talking to my own soul." Out of that sharing grows the

---

[33] *Twenty One Love Poems* (Emeryville, California: Effie's Press, 1976).

ability to chose solitude "without loneliness," to define one's own sphere of action and growth:

> I choose to be a figure in that light,
> half-blotted by darkness, something moving
> across that space, the color of stone
> greeting the moon, yet more than stone:
> a woman. I choose to walk here. And to draw this circle.

The choice, here and in most of Adrienne Rich's poetry, is of a process, a way of becoming, rather than a narrowly defined end.

That emphasis on process can also be found in her frequent images of women creating beautiful quilts out of small pieces of fabric and experience that many women have made, saved and cherished, "Piecing our lore in quilted galaxies," as she says in "Sibling Mysteries." In "Natural Resources" she gathers up "these things by women saved,"

> these ribboned letters, snapshots
>
> faithfully glued for years
> onto the scrapbook page
>
> these scraps, turned into patchwork.

and the effort is the poet's attempt to give women back the past that has been lost to us, a past of "humble things" without which we have "no memory / no faithfulness, no purpose for the future / no honor to the past." She tells us it is against this knowledge of other women that we must now analyze and test our perceptions and visions for the future.

Adrienne Rich was once accused of "the will to be contemporary," an unhappy influence on her poetry, as she was "neither a radical innovator nor the voice of an age."[34] She is, in fact, both. No poet's voice has spoken as hers has in this period of profound social change in the relations between women and men, among women themselves. In the nearly three decades in which Adrienne Rich has been writing poetry, the quality of her vision and of her poems has been unique. We find again in these poems

> . . . no mere will to mastery,
> only care for the many-lived, unending
> forms in which she finds herself.

---

[34] Boyers, p.144.

Her voice and her work are distinguished by a commitment to "the fibers of actual life" and to change, a commitment that is unmatched in her poetic generation.

I have to cast my lot with those
who age after age, perversely,

with no extraordinary power,
reconstitute the world.